W9-BME-817

Volcanoes

Shar Levine and Leslie Johnstone

SL:
For LJ – Congratulations on finishing your
Masters. Now we can get back to serious work.

LJ:
For Shar – You constantly amaze me...
and in a good way.

Volcanoes
by Shar Levine and Leslie Johnston

Copyright © 2007, 2010 by
Mud Puddle Books, Inc.
36 W. 25th Street
5th Floor
New York, NY 10016
info@mudpuddlebooks.com

ISBN: 978-1-60311-062-4

All rights reserved. No part of this book may be reproduced or transmitted
in any form or by any means, electronic or mechanical, including
photocopying, recording, or by any information storage and
retrieval system, without permission in writing from the publisher.

Printed in China

The authors are grateful for the assistance of Rob Rainbird, Ph. D., Geological Survey of Canada – Natural Resources Canada, and Teresa Wilson. We would also like to thank Art MacKenzie for taking time in April to matchmake us with Rob.

INTRODUCTION

Close your eyes and think of a volcano. Do you see something shaped like an upside down ice cream cone with the pointed part bitten off? There are volcanoes that look like this but they can be other shapes too.

Volcanoes can be found on land, under the ocean and on our moon. They have even been found on other planets and on their moons.

Obviously this book can't teach you everything there is to know about volcanoes, but you will learn the basics about this exciting subject.

A volcano

WHAT'S BELOW YOUR FEET?

If you were able to drill a hole to the center of the earth, this is what you would find:

First you would drill through the rocky crust. Much like the peel covering an apple, Earth's outer layer or crust is the thinnest layer. The crust can be as little as 3 miles (5 km) thick under the ocean and as much as 45 miles (70 km) thick under some mountains. The crust is made up of large sections called plates. Where the crust is covered by oceans, it is known as oceanic crust and where it forms the land, it is known as the continental crust.

Beneath the crust is the mantle, which is a solid and liquid layer about 1,800 miles (2,900 km) thick. The outer part of the mantle is called the lithosphere, and it forms the lower layer of the Earth's plates. The lower part of the mantle, the asthenosphere, is a thick, moving fluid of melted rock that rises and falls as it heats and cools. This motion is thought to move the large plates making up the crust.

At the very center of the earth is the core which is made up of two parts. The liquid

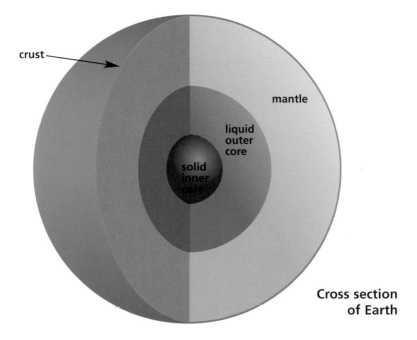

crust

mantle

liquid outer core

solid inner core

Cross section of Earth

outer core is about 1,400 miles (2,200 km) thick and is made of melted metal. The solid inner core is about 800 miles (1,300 km) in diameter and is thought to be made of the metals iron and nickel. No one has ever seen this as it is about 4,000 miles (6,400 km) straight down from the place you are standing.

Did you know?

Special drilling equipment can be used to make holes a long way into the crust but no one has yet reached the mantle below.

WHAT IS A VOLCANO?

Volcanoes are hills and mountains that are formed from magma, which is melted rock from Earth's mantle coming up through cracks in the Earth's crust. The word volcano is used to describe the opening in the crust where the magma comes out. When the magma comes out or erupts onto the surface, it is called lava. When the lava turns solid it can be called volcanic rock. The most common volcanic rocks are basalt, andesite and rhyolite.

Magma contains gases such as water vapor and carbon dioxide. If the magma is thick these gases become trapped and can come out very quickly, causing explosive results! If you shook a sealed bottle of soda pop, then uncapped it, the contents would

Did you know?

"Lava" is from the Italian word meaning "to slide", while "Magma" comes from the Italian word for a thick material.

explode then pour out of the bottle. This is similar to what happens when a volcano erupts. Volcanoes formed from thicker magma release the gases more easily and have gentler lava flows.

WHAT CAUSES VOLCANOES?

The crust of the earth was not always the way it is today. In the past the Earth's plates were in different positions.

Scientists explain this using the theory of plate tectonics. According to this theory, the plates that make up the crust are always moving, pushed along by the flow of the fluid lower part of the mantle underneath the plates. The fluid mantle is heated by the core and then rises, and spreads outward. As it spreads, it cools and sinks back down into the lower mantle where it is heated up again forming a loop called a convection current. The outward spreading of the current carries the overlying plate with it.

Volcanoes form in the areas where two plates come close to each other. In these loca-tions, the plates can either move together and

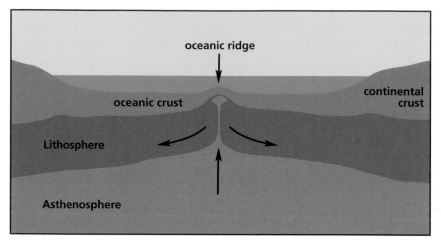

Ocean ridge volcano

one can move beneath the other, or they move apart. When one plate moves beneath another it is called subduction.

Ridges form in the middle of oceans where two plates move apart. Magma moves up between the plates forming new rock on the ocean floor. Volcanoes that form along the ridge can form islands that rise out of the ocean. Iceland is an example of an ocean ridge volcano.

When plates move apart on land a rift is formed. A rift is a crack in the crust along which volcanoes can form. One example where this occurs is the Great Rift Valley in East Africa.

In areas where there is subduction and one plate moves beneath the other, the subducting plate is pushed so far down into the mantle that it heats up and melts. This melted rock or magma is under lots of pressure and can cause large volcanic eruptions.

When two oceanic plates collide and one subducts beneath the other, volcanoes form a curved chain of island scalled a volcanic arc. This is what happened to form such island countries as Japan, Indonesia, and the Philippines.

Volcanoes are also formed where oceanic crust subducts or moves under the continental crust. These volcanoes form chains of coastal mountains, such as those found on the west coast of North and South America.

Subduction

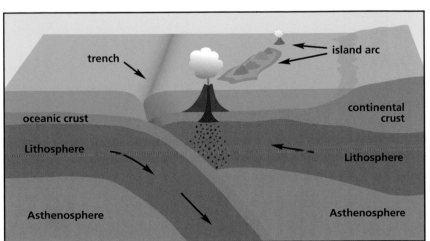

HOT SPOTS

Most volcanoes occur at the edges of the plates that make up the earth's crust but there are a few places on the earth where volcanoes occur in the middle of a plate. These volcanoes are formed from hot upwellings from the Earth's mantle called hot spots.

Hot spots form when hot magma rises up and melts through the Earth's crust. The magma erupts and forms a volcano. As the

Hawaiian isles and hot spot

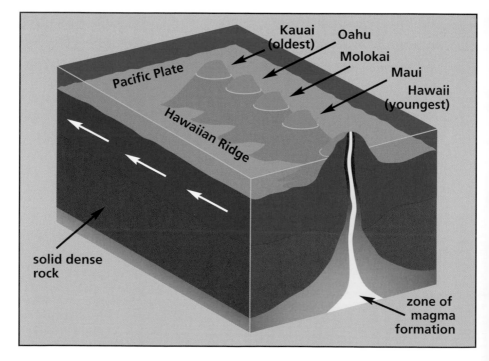

plate continues to move over the hot spot more volcanoes are made.

This eventually produces a string of volcanoes that line up along the direction of the plate movement. The volcanoes will be in order of their age with the oldest one farthest from the hot spot.

The Hawaiian Islands are a good example of a string of volcanoes formed by a hot spot. Kauai would have been the first island to form, followed by Oahu, Molokai and Maui. Hawaii is the youngest of the islands and it is home to the active volcanoes Kilauea and Mauna Loa.

A small piece of the Earth's oceanic crust, called ophiolite, has recently been discovered in Greenland. Scientists are excited by this find because the rock is 3.8 billion years old and so the Earth's plates are more than a billion years older than earlier thought.

WHAT IS INSIDE A VOLCANO?

The hole in the center of a volcano is called a vent. Sheets of magma that cut across the layers of volcanoes are called dikes. If layers of magma form or intrude along the layers of the volcano they are called sills. Sometimes dikes will break through to the surface forming an eruption on the side of the volcano.

Some volcanoes have bowl-shaped craters at their top. Smaller craters are usually caused by the volcanic eruption. Larger craters called calderas are formed when the top parts of volcanoes collapse following an eruption.

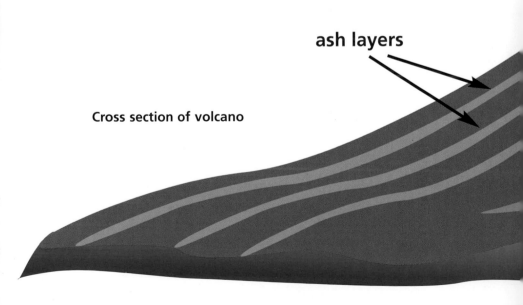

ash layers

Cross section of volcano

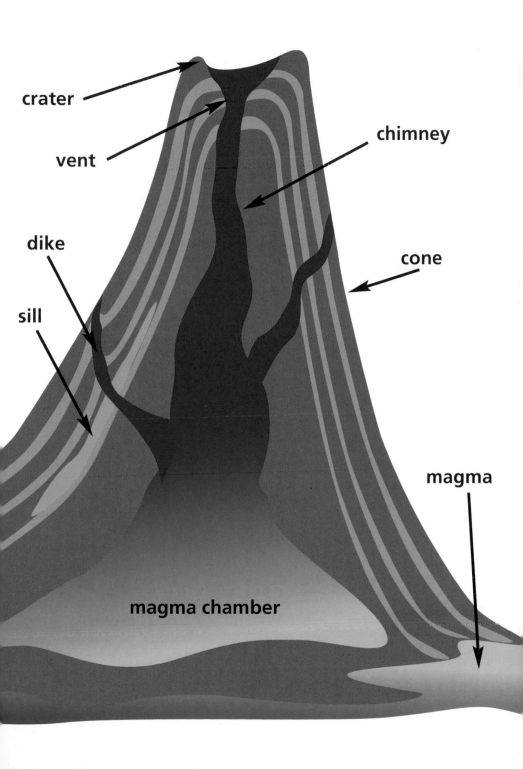

crater

vent

chimney

dike

cone

sill

magma

magma chamber

TYPES OF VOLCANOES

Not all volcanoes look the same. They can be different shapes and sizes. There are a number of ways of classifying or describing volcanoes.

Cinder cones are the simplest kind of volcano. They have one vent going up the middle, filled with lava that has collected and solidified. As it erupts, this volcano sends lava up into the air. The lava cools quickly and breaks into small pieces that fall back into and around volcanoes. The explosive

Cross section of cone volcano

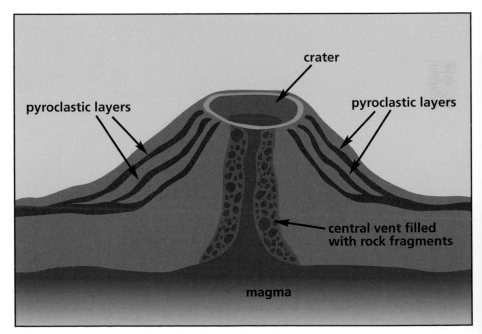

crater

pyroclastic layers

pyroclastic layers

central vent filled with rock fragments

magma

eruption makes a crater around the vent that looks like a bowl. These volcanoes aren't very tall and may be about 1,000 feet (300 m) from the base to the top.

Unlike the cinder cone volcano, a shield volcano has many thin tubes from which the lava can erupt. Shield volcanoes have gentle slopes and are made up of layers of lava which have flowed into a shape that looks like an ancient warrior's shield laid flat. Mauna Loa on the island of Hawaii is the largest shield volcano.

Cross section of shield volcano

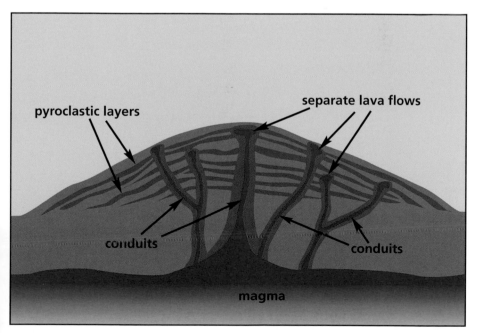

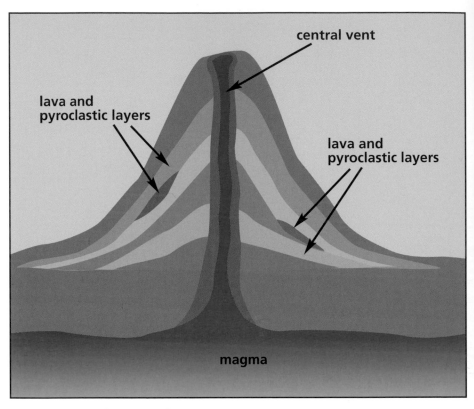

Cross section of stratovolcano

The most common type of volcano is the stratovolcano or composite volcano. Like their name suggests, they are made up of different layers. These layers are formed from lava that has erupted from a vent or tube in the center of the volcano. Stratovolcanoes form mountains like Mount Fuji in Japan or

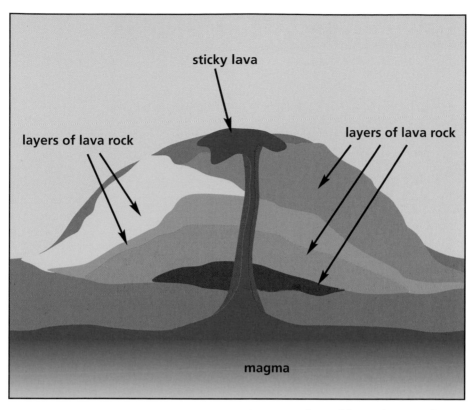

Cross section of lava dome volcano

Mount St. Helen's in the United States. While they are very pretty to look at, they are also the most deadly.

Some of the other types of volcanoes include compound volcanoes, lava domes, somma volcanoes, tuff cones, fissure volcanoes and table mountains.

SUBMARINE VOLCANOES

Some islands are formed from volcanic activity deep under the ocean. These submarine volcanoes do not act the same way they do on land. You would think that the cold ocean water would extinguish or put out any hot lava that might flow from the volcano, but that doesn't exactly happen.

If the volcano is close to the surface of the water, the lava may turn the water into steam and rocks formed from cooling of the lava may be thrown high into the air. If the volcano is deep under ocean, the weight or pressure of the water stops the volcano from erupting violently.

Imagine what "Old Faithful", the hot steam geyser at Yellowstone National Park, would look like underwater. This is what a hydrothermal or hot water vent looks like at the bottom of the ocean. Minerals in the hot water crystallize or grow together to create tall, hollow tubes called "Black Smokers."

? Would you like to live next to an active volcano?

Scientists have discovered strange sea creatures that make their home near hydrothermal chimneys, or volcanic steam vents at the bottom of the ocean. The Pompeii worm (*Alvinella pompejana*) is one such creature that doesn't seem to mind that the temperature of the water is almost boiling.

The Pompeii worm

THAR SHE BLOWS!

When you see a volcano erupt in a movie or on a TV show, the ground shakes, giant rocks are thrown through the air, rushing lava flows down the mountain, and cars are covered in a thick layer of ash. The bad guy is swallowed up by a crater, and the hero escapes. But what really happens? Volcanoes erupt when magma forces its way up to the surface. They erupt explosively when the magma and the gases it contains escape very quickly through a small vent.

Itsy Bitsy Volcanoes

Scientists have recently identified "petit-spot" or small volcanoes. These volcanoes were discovered by Naota Hirano and unlike traditional volcanoes they are not located at the edge of plates or on "hot spots." Although they are described as small, even the smallest ones would be about the size of a football stadium.

22

Not all volcanoes have rivers of lava oozing down their sides, but if there is lava, it generally moves along at a speed where people can run away. Still, lava is burning hot, and will destroy trees, homes, and anything that does not move out of its way.

You may know the Hawaiian word for "hello" is *Aloha,* and that a flower necklace is called a Lei, but did you know that the Hawaiian language has given us the words for describing basaltic lava, the most common kind of lava?

A'a (ah-ah) is thick, fast moving lava that has a rough or sharp surface when it hardens. *Pahoehoe* (pahoweehowee) is thin, slow moving lava that looks smooth and shiny when it hardens.

Pillow lava forms where lava flows or erupts into water. Like its name, this lava looks like giant fat pillows squeezed from the ground as if it were toothpaste from a tube.

There are other kinds of lava too, including, Andesitic, Dacitic, and Rhyolitic lavas.

Obviously you cannot stick a thermometer into erupting lava to measure its temperature. A safe way to estimate the temperature of lava is to look at its color. The hotter the temperature, the more yellow the color of the lava and the cooler the temperature, the more red the lava will be. Lava can be over 900 degrees C or 1,650 degrees F.

Hawaiians call thinly spun lava "Pele's Hair", while lava shaped like water drops is called "Pele's Tears."

GAS

While it is easy to escape from a lava flow, gases from volcanoes are deadly. Poisonous gases such as carbon dioxide, sink to the ground, and kill any creature that breathes them. Hydrogen sulfide, a gas that smells like rotten eggs, and other acidic gases including sulfur dioxide make your eyes water and your throat burn. The gases don't always blow away. Some dissolve in lakes and streams, creating water that is so acidic it would burn your skin.

In 1986, 1,700 people were killed, and hundreds more were injured, by carbon dioxide gas released at Lake Nyos in Africa.

ASH

If you look at the ash in a fireplace, you wouldn't think that something so fine could be dangerous. But fiery ash from a volcanic eruption can bury entire towns in a matter of hours. As dissolved gases in the magma expand, it explodes into rock fragments called pyroclasts that vary in size from a speck of dust to as big as a house. The fine dust is called volcanic ash. When the fragments have cooled they are called tephra and they can cover a huge area. Volocanic ash can be carried by wind for thousands of miles away from the volcano it came from.

Pompeii and Herculaneum

When Mount Vesuvius erupted about 2,000 years ago it covered the towns of Pompeii and Herculaneum several yards (meters) deep in ash. This ancient site was excavated about 100 years ago, revealing what life was like at the time of the eruption. Food, household items, people, and even the family dog are all perfectly preserved in time. From body positions of the dead people, you can see that they tried to hide to protect themselves from the volcanic ash.

Pompeii

Pompeii

Lava isn't the only thing which can flow down a volcano after it erupts. Mud, and other debris, such as trees or rocks, can come barreling down a slope, taking with it anything in its way.

Mount St. Helens, Washington State

When Mount St. Helens erupted in 1980, the hot pyroclastic materials melted the snow and ice on the mountain's top causing a powerful debris and mudflow. The hot flow traveled down the slopes at over 90 miles per hour (144 km per hour), taking with it just about everything in its path.

THE BIGGER PICTURE

Very large eruptions can affect the atmosphere around the world. Tsunamis, earthquakes and ash clouds associated with volcanic eruptions can affect places far away from the volcano.

Krakatau

One volcanic eruption that had widespread results was the 1883 eruption of the Krakatau volcano in Indonesia. This violent eruption caused tsunamis with waves over 100 feet (30 m) high that destroyed cities and towns on the coast. Over 36,000 people were killed by these waves. The eruption was heard more than 3,000 miles (4,800 km) away in Australia. Shockwaves from the eruption traveled around the Earth three times. Ash in the atmosphere from the eruption caused a lower average temperature world-wide for the next three years.

TYPES OF ERUPTIONS

Volcanoes in some areas of the world are very dangerous when they erupt. In other areas people live near volcanoes with very little danger. What makes volcanoes dangerous is volcanic eruption. There are several different types of volcanic eruption.

Icelandic-type eruptions are quite gentle. Hawaiian eruptions make streams of hot liquid lava that escape from a vent.

Strombolian-type eruptions are formed from thicker lava that causes more violent eruptions. During these eruptions small lumps of hot lava and cinders can shoot out into the air. Vulcanian eruptions are similar to Strombolian eruptions but are even more violent.

Pelean eruptions are also similar but they involve avalanches of hot ash that pour out from the vent at high speed. These avalanches can be followed by more violent explosions.

Plinian-type eruptions are the most violent. During these eruptions hot lava, ash and gases can shoot more than 12 miles (19 km) into the air.

WHERE TO FIND A VOLCANO

Just about everywhere you look on Earth, you can find a volcano. From deep under the ice in Iceland, to remote islands in the Pacific Ocean, you can find these features. It is estimated that there have been 1,500 volcanoes that have erupted over the last 10,000 years.

If you are hunting for volcanoes, the best place to look is around the "ring of fire", a chain of volcanic islands around the edge of the Pacific Ocean. This is where the majority of Earth's present-day eruptions occur.

Ring of fire

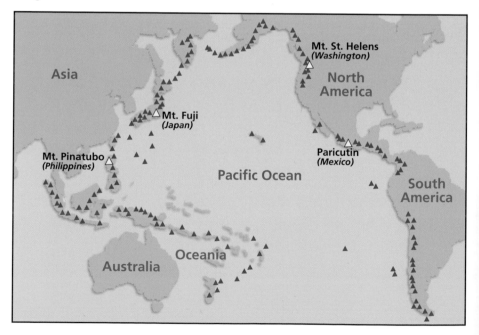

LIVE, DEAD, OR DORMANT

Volcanoes are called live if they are still erupting. Volcanoes that are not erupting are called either dormant or dead. Dormant volcanoes still have some form of activity, like steam or hot springs. They could still become active in the future. If a volcano is extinct it is thought to no longer have any volcanic activity at all and it is not expected to ever erupt again.

Which is higher— Mount Everest or Mauna Kea?

While it's true that the highest point on Earth is Mount Everest at 29,000 feet (8,850 meters) above sea level, Mauna Kea's base is on the bottom of the ocean, meaning that it is actually 32,000 feet (9,750 meters) from its bottom to the top.

VOLCANOES ON OTHER PLANETS

Let's go on a volcano hunt around our solar system. Our first stop is the Earth's moon. There aren't any live or dormant volcanoes on our moon, but the moon has small basaltic cinder cones and volcanic domes. This means that at some time in the past there were active volcanoes.

The volcanoes on Mars are very old, between 3 and 4 billion years old! On a trip to Mars you wouldn't find many volcanoes but among the ones you did find would be the largest shield volcanoes in the solar system. These dormant volcanoes are more than three times higher than Mauna Kea, and you would need to have 100 Hawaiian volcanoes added together to equal the diameter of a Martian volcano. Martian volcanoes appear to be created by hot spots. Mars doesn't seem to have the types of volcanoes seen at the edges of moving crustal plates.

If you really want to see volcanoes, and have your own spaceship, then Venus would be your best bet. This planet has more volcanoes than anywhere else in our solar system.

Io and Jupiter

Venus has so many volcanic features that no one has ever counted them all. And, while most of these volcanoes appear to be extinct, scientists think there may still be some that are live or dormant.

On Io, one of the moons of Jupiter, you will find the most volcanic activity in our solar system. Images from the Galileo Probe and from the NASA Infrared Telescope Facility show spectacular eruptions on this moon.

VOLCANO GODS AND LEGENDS

People in ancient times did not understand the science behind volcanoes. Instead, they thought that there were gods controlling the eruptions. Each place had its own legend surrounding a volcano.

In Hawaii, Pele was the goddess of fire, lightning, dance and volcanoes. She was always fighting with her sister, the goddess of water. When Pele was angry she caused erup-

According to Hawaiian legend, it is bad luck to take a piece of lava away from the island. Tourists who have ignored this superstition frequently send back bits they have stolen with letters explaining all the terrible luck they had after leaving Hawaii. This "legend" may be modern, as some locals claim that a park ranger invented it to stop tourists from taking lava samples.

Volcano names and Mr. Spock

So what do volcanoes and Star Trek's Mr. Spock have in common? If you are a fan of the original television series, you will remember that Spock's home was Vulcan, a fiery planet with active volcanoes.

The creators of the program were inspired by "Vulcan", the Roman god of blacksmiths and volcanoes. Smoke from a volcano on the small island of Vulcano, near Italy, was thought to be the chimney of this god.

tions. Hawaiians still give offerings at Kilauea Volcano on the island of Hawaii.

Mt. Fuji, in Japan, was the home of the goddess Sengen, who was said to throw people who weren't worthy of worshiping her off the mountain.

In New Zealand, they believed that the volcanoes Taranaki and Ruapehu were male giants and that Tongariro was a female giant.

The two male giants fought for the love of the woman by throwing stones and boiling water at each other.

When a volcano in Iceland erupted nearly a thousand years ago, people thought that the Hekla volcano was an entrance to Hell. The sound made by the volcano was thought to be people crying in the underworld.

VIEWING VOLCANOES

The best place to see a volcano is from the safety of your own home. Many government web sites feature photographs, and videos of volcanic eruptions. Of course you could always visit Kilauea, on the big island of Hawaii, where you have an opportunity to see lava flowing in the ocean, or walk on the flat caldera next to puffs of steam that still rise from the surface.

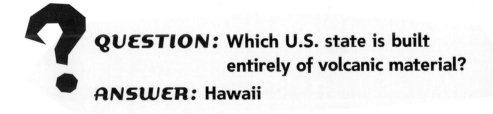

QUESTION: Which U.S. state is built entirely of volcanic material?

ANSWER: Hawaii

? What can you do with a dormant volcano?

High atop of the dormant Hawaiian volcano of Mauna Kea, you will find some of the world's most powerful space observatories. The star-gazing facilities are located at nearly 14,000 ft above sea level (4,205 meters). The extremely thin atmosphere is also dry and usually free from clouds. The remote location means lights from the city do not brighten the sky. This makes the viewing of far off galaxies easier than using telescopes located closer to the ground or nearer cities. These observatories have web sites that show you what they are viewing that night.

Observatory

CAN VOLCANOES BE A GOOD THING?

So far in this book you have only read about the bad things that can happen when volcanoes erupt. But can volcanoes ever serve a useful purpose?

Geothermal power is created using the heat from volcanic areas. In places such as Iceland and New Zealand, this kind of energy heats homes and makes electricity. Geothermal energy is good for the environment and does not use up any materials.

Valuable metallic minerals such as copper, gold, silver, zinc and lead are formed when small amounts of these elements are concentrated in the liquid magma. This will eventually produce enough of the metal that it can be

Did you know?

Pumice, a light, air-filled type of volcanic rock is used by the cosmetic industry as a natural way to scrub rough spots from people's skin.

Enormous crystals

When minerals cool quickly they form tiny crystals, but slower cooling results in the formation of large crystals. One place you can see this is the Cave of Crystals in Mexico's volcanic Naica Mountain. Huge crystals of gypsum that are up to 36 feet (11 m) long and have estimated weights of up to 55 tons formed over hundreds of thousands of years. The heat from the volcano allowed the mineral to very slowly form crystals.

mined. Gemstones, such as diamonds, rubies, opals and sapphires are also mined from some types of volcanic rock.

While the ash and lava look pretty unusable, they eventually weather down to a rich and fertile soil, which is perfect for growing food crops and lush forests. Some of the most fertile regions on Earth are lands that were once near an active volcano.

Volcanic glass

When magma cools very quickly it forms tiny crystals. Obsidian, or volcanic glass, is created when the magma cools so fast that no crystals form at all. This volcanic glass was used for making cutting tools and weapons by early people.

IS THIS ANY WAY TO MAKE A LIVING?

If you'd like to work in a really hot field, you could become a volcanologist; a scientist who studies volcanoes. Wearing special fire and heat resistant suits, these brave scientists, collect samples of lava and gas, and take measurements documenting the volcanic activity. They make use of instruments such as seismometers that measure small gound shakings, called tremors, that occur before some eruptions. Lasers are also used to measure small amounts of movement in the Earth's crust.

Scientists use all kinds of scales for measuring natural phenomena. Earthquakes are measured using the Richter scale, and wind speed is calculated using the Beaufort scale. The intensity of a volcanic eruption can be rated on the Volcanic Explosivity Index or VEI which describes eruptions. It is too dangerous to attach a measuring device to an erupting volcano, so instead characteristics of the volcano such as the frequency and height of the eruption are used.

NEW VOLCANOES

One of the exciting things about volcanoes is that you never know where one will pop up next! In August, 2006, the crew aboard the yacht, Maiken, witnessed the strangest sight. The blue ocean they were sailing in began to be covered with floating pumice. It looked as if the water had turned into a sandy beach. As they traveled through this, they saw a volcano erupt in the distance, and rise from the ocean's floor. The crew witnessed the birth of a new island in the South Pacific. This place does not have a name and it may not be around too long. It is classified as an "ephemeral" island, meaning that wind and waves will erode the land until it disappears in several years.

Breaking News!

Scientists in Florida using satellite radar imagery have designed a new technique to predict eruptions based on swellings or bulges on the sides of volcanoes. Researchers hope to apply this model in the future to forecast explosions.

A'a (ah-ah) – lava that has a rough or sharp surface when it hardens

Andesite – a type of fine grained volcanic rock

Ash – fine powdery volcanic lava

Asthenosphere – the lower liquid part of the mantle

Basalt – a dark fine grained volcanic rock commonly found in lava flows

Caldera – large bowl shaped depression at the top of a volcano

Cinder Cones – a simple type of volcano with only one vent

Core – the very center part of the earth; the inner core is solid, while the outer core is liquid

Craters – a bowl-shaped area on the top of the volcano

Crust – a rocky layer covering the earth

Dead Volcano – a volcano that has no activity and is not expected to erupt

Dikes – Sheets of magma that cut across the layers of volcanoes

Dormant Volcano – a volcano that is not erupting but still shows activity ie. steam

Eruption – when lava bursts out of a volcano

Gases – the fluid state of matter that can expand indefinitely. Gases that come from volcanoes include carbon dioxide and water vapour.

Geothermal Power – using heat from a volcano for power

Hot Spot – An area that forms when hot magma rises up and melts through the rocks making up the crust.

Lahar – a mud slide that happens down the side of a volcano

Lava – magma that has come to the surface

Lithosphere – upper part of the mantle

Live Volcano – a volcano that is still erupting

Magma – melted rock under the earth

Mantle – a solid and liquid layer beneath the Earth's crust

Ophiolite – a rock formation found in Earth's crust

Pahoehoe (pah-hoy-hoy) – is thin, slow moving lava that looks smooth and shiny when it hardens.

Pillow Lava – lava formed under water or where lava enters the ocean

Plate Tectonics – scientific explanation of the movement of the plates

Plates – sections of the crust and lithosphere

Pyroclastics – rock material made into fragments through volcanic action

Rhyolite – a common rock that makes up the magma and lava

Ring of Fire – an area around the Pacific Ocean where the majority of Earth's eruptions occur.

Shield Volcano – a type of volcano with gentle slopes

Sills – layers of magma that has formed across the volcano

Stratovolcano – most common type of volcano-also called a composite volcano

Subduction – when one plate moves below another plate

Submarine Volcano – a volcano under water

Tephra – cooled fragments of pyroclastics

Tsunami – a large wave caused by a volcanic eruption or an earthquake

Vent – the center hole in the volcano from which Magma rises

Volcanoes – hills or mountains that are formed from melted rock deep inside the earth coming up to the Earth's crust or the opening in the crust where the melted rock comes out.

Volcano Explosive Index – a way of rating volcanic eruptions

Volcanologist – a scientist who studies volcanoes

PHOTO CREDITS

pg.　5: Volcano photo © Angelo Vianello/istockphoto
International

pg. 21: Deep sea Pompeii worm photo
© deepseaphotography.com

pg. 26: Pompeii, top photo © D. Huss/istockphoto
International

pg. 26: Pompeii, bottom photo © Branislav Bubanja/
istockphoto International

pg. 33: Io and Jupiter photo © Clark Dunbar/Corbis

pg. 37: Observatory photo © Shar Levine